Adventures in Healthcare

By

Daniel Bonk

Disclaimer

Copyright © the Year 2023

All Rights Reserved.

No part of this eBook can be transmitted or reproduced in any form, including print, electronic, photocopying, scanning, mechanical, or recording, without prior written permission from the author.

While the author has made utmost efforts to ensure the accuracy of the written content, all readers are advised to follow the information mentioned herein at their own risk. The author cannot be held responsible for any personal or commercial damage caused by misinterpretation of information. All readers are encouraged to seek professional advice when needed.

This eBook has been written for information purposes only. Every effort has been made to make this eBook as complete and accurate as possible. However, there may be mistakes in typography or content. Also, this e-book provides information only up to the publishing date. Therefore, this eBook should be used as a guide - not as the ultimate source.

The purpose of this eBook is to educate. The author and the publisher do not warrant that the information contained in this eBook is fully complete and shall not be responsible for any errors or omissions. The author and publisher shall have neither liability nor responsibility to any person or entity with respect to any loss or damage caused or alleged to be caused directly or indirectly by this e-book.

Table of Contents

Introduction

Healthcare, a profession often thought of as solemn, marked by grave circumstances, isn't as serious as it is commonly perceived.

Join me on a journey in *Adventures in Healthcare*, spanning four decades in healthcare leadership, where serious matters meet unexpected twists. The book is a collection of some of my very own unforgettable anecdotes, some very serious, others hilarious or unbelievable.

Amidst the pages of this book, you'll get to see a different side of healthcare, celebrating the joyous moments, the unexpected experiences, and the bizarre incidents that inevitably unfold amidst the serious business of healing.

Enjoy the unique and engaging adventures that await you, and remember that sometimes, the best stories emerge from the most unexpected places.

Wishing you good health!

-     Daniel Bonk

Unleashed Emotions: Throwing a Scalpel

Working in a hospital can be quite stressful. Even so, we are trained to control our emotions, and we practice that control every day. It is important for us to remember that we are in this line of work to prioritize the well-being of our patients, families, communities, and each other. But truth be told, on rare occasions, even we, with all the training and practice, can't control our emotions at times. And when such an incident occurs, it results in the person in question being removed from the patient care environment.

I remember one incident very clearly. Our hospital had recently welcomed a new surgical group to our medical staff. Since they were from another state, their history was relatively unknown to us, apart from the basic credentials.

One morning, my Chief of Surgery approached me with a situation that sent my blood pressure off the chart. A surgeon, feeling frustrated with the perceived slowness of his surgical team, threw a scalpel at one of the nurses in the operating room, hitting her shoulder. Thankfully, the scalpel didn't cause any injury, but the act itself was unacceptable and warranted immediate action.

I immediately went to see the surgeon just as he was on his way to leave the hospital. I forcibly escorted him to my office and requested the presence of my Chief Medical Officer to address the situation.

I informed the surgeon that his privileges were suspended until further notice, and he was not to return to the hospital until the issue was formally resolved.

The physician got belligerent, trying to justify his actions. But what was really annoying me during this heated argument was a constant knocking at my door that I was trying to ignore. Having had enough of the noise (both inside and out), I finally got up and opened the door. My Chief Operating Officer was standing there impatiently and told me she needed to talk with me immediately. I pointed to the surgeon, still screaming at my Chief Medical Officer, and told her I was obviously in the middle of this mess and didn't have the time. Well, she didn't accept that answer and literally dragged me by my tie into the hallway. There, she pointed down the hall where I saw a very large, very muscular, and *very* angry man talking to the head of our Human Resources department.

It turned out this very large and very angry man was, of course, the husband of the nurse who was struck by the scalpel, and he was there on a mission: to take out the doctor who tossed the scalpel at his wife!

 Fortunately, I was able to slip back to my office, letting my Chief Operating Officer and HR director deal with the angry husband, keeping him at bay. After I went back, I sat down, turned to the surgeon, and uttered what might just be the best line I've had the chance to say in my 40 years of being a hospital leader; I told him, "Doctor, I'm not your worst problem today."

Against my better judgment, I allowed the surgeon to exit the hospital through another door. He literally disappeared. No one ever saw him again. The rumor was that he had returned to his native country.

Apologies and Ashes: The Duffel Bag Surprise

In a notable chapter of my career within a for-profit health system, I had the privilege of serving in three distinct roles. Firstly, I held the position of CEO in a hospital. Additionally, I took on the responsibility of being a corporate ethics instructor for the entire system. Lastly, I found myself frequently alongside a physician colleague evaluating hospitals where CEOs had quit or been terminated. We would usually be in the facility for 30 to 40 days. Throughout my career, I believe I engaged in this evaluation process in approximately a dozen hospitals within the health system.

So, on my very first day at a sprawling hospital in Texas, I was approached by the Chief Nursing Officer, the Director of Risk Management, and the Chief Medical Officer.

Well, this certainly can't be good, was the first thing that popped into my mind.

They asked me to meet with the family of a patient who had received what some felt was inadequate care. The patient had died in the hospital's care...

The request was for me, as the Chief Executive Officer, to apologize in hopes that this would dissuade the family from pursuing any sort of legal action against the hospital.

I agreed to meet with the family. I did not have the details of the case yet, but I thought of it as a simple enough task. After all, how hard could apologizing be? At that point in my career, I felt I was an expert apologizer. I could apologize to anyone!

Two days later, the spouse and the son of the patient who had died came to meet me in my office. As we gathered around a round conference table, I couldn't help but notice that the son, who appeared to be in his mid-20s, had brought along a duffel bag, which I thought was a bit odd and concerning at the same time.

But I decided to shrug it off and not let it bother me as I introduced myself and began to express my condolences. However, before I could get very far, the patient's spouse raised her hand to cut me off and said something that left me baffled to the very core.

"Don't apologize to us; apologize to him."

At that moment, the son unzipped the duffel bag and carefully retrieved an urn, placing it solemnly on the table. The wife requested that I direct my apology to her husband, whose ashes now rested within the urn on the table.

Dumbfounded, I shifted my gaze to the urn sitting on the table and proceeded to apologize to it. It would be safe to say the encounter left an indelible mark on my memory.

Later that afternoon, I called my boss and said that I needed a raise. After that day, I never followed up regarding lawsuits with that organization and have not apologized to another urn since.

Ethics Unveiled: Meeting the FBI and Justice Department

For a short period during my career, I found myself involved in the establishment of freestanding rehabilitation hospitals. However, I had a strong desire to transition back into acute care. It was at this point that a large for-profit health system reached out to me with an intriguing proposition: if I financially turned around one of their rehabilitation hospitals within their system, they would then facilitate my move into an acute care facility.

On my third day at the rehabilitation hospital, an unexpected fax arrived from the FBI (no kidding, unexpected) warning us against the destruction of any documents under the threat of fines and potential imprisonment.

Later that day, we learned that about 40 FBI agents had raided the corporate office of the health system, unearthing (alleged) wrongdoings in various parts of the organization. Subsequently, the health system reached an agreement with the Justice Department, agreeing to pay fines close to one billion dollars. Patients and families had also filed millions of dollars in civil suits. In addition, they were required to implement a robust ethics program, establish an ethics hotline, and enforce stringent guidelines for all leadership positions. As part of the agreement, senior leadership personnel, including myself, were summoned to meet with the Justice Department, where we were informed that future illegal and some unethical behaviors would be prosecuted under the RICO statutes rather than being handled as they had been in the past.

Several months later, I was transferred from the rehabilitation hospital to an acute care facility within the health system.

I took on the added role of corporate integrity officer. As mandated by the agreement with the Justice Department, all employees were required to receive one-hour ethics training in order to be scheduled to work. Having previously engaged in ethics work, I was among the few CEOs selected to facilitate this training.

I did this training in over 20 of our hospitals. The first question I was always asked was, "Why do we have to sit through this?"

I always started with the corporate response, "It will help us be better community citizens," "This ethics program will make us stronger," "This is part of our mission," etc. When pushed, I would often follow up with what I felt was the real answer: "You can only pay one 900 million dollar fine and survive, and jail is also not an option.

Shattered Reflection: Counseling Turns Bloody

Very early in my career, I worked as a health educator at a closed-panel HMO. My responsibilities included conducting individual and group health education sessions. I also collaborated with a psychiatric social worker to lead a weight loss program group, where I focused on providing information about the specifics of calorie reduction and exercises while the social worker addressed the psychological issues linked to weight loss.

Within this group, there was a mother and daughter who were QUITE heavy. When weighing the mother before class, in order to get an accurate weight, I had to add an additional weight to the top of the scale because her weight exceeded the scale's maximum capacity.

Over the course of three consecutive classes, the mother submitted food logs indicating that she was consuming less than 1500 calories per day, yet she continued to gain weight.

Despite undergoing numerous metabolic and other tests to explore potential physiological reasons for her inability to lose weight, no underlying issues were discovered.

So, one day after class, I asked the mother to wait so that I could discuss her food logs with her. As she sat on the couch, I walked closer to her to show empathy. When I did so, she admitted that she was not keeping her food logs accurately. So, to further establish empathy and better communication and search for a solution, I moved to sit on a glass coffee table near where she was seated on the couch. Not surprisingly, that was a mistake.

Just as I sat on the table, the glass literally exploded, and I fell into it. I could feel shards of glass in different parts of my body. I struggled to pull myself up and then quickly pulled the glass out of my rear and my shoulders, all the while still standing in the middle of the destroyed table. I'm sure that was not a pretty sight.

After pulling out the larger pieces of glass, I looked at my hands; they were covered in blood. It was then that I looked up at the mother, who had stood up when I fell and, at that exact moment, passed out, falling directly on top of me. And you can guess what happened next. That's right; I fell back into the destroyed table and the shattered glass. I then rolled her off me (keeping her off the glass), and at that point, the clinic staff came running into the room because, as I was later told, they thought that a gunshot had gone off in the conference room.

There was just one more thing; the mother was, well, very – well endowed, and as I was attempting to catch her as she fell, my palms landed on her chest, leaving bloody handprints on the front of her white blouse. Thankfully, she was not hurt in any way, but she was left traumatized by the experience! (she was not the only one !).

As for my injuries, I received 12 stitches in my shoulder and 14 stitches in my backside.

Several months later, I took another opportunity, and when I prepared to leave the clinic, the team had a going away party for me. As I unwrapped one of my going-away presents, there it was – a framed white blouse with "bloody" (ketchup) handprints on the front.

Guardians: Code Pink

Hospitals conduct various types of drills, encompassing patient safety, inclement weather, natural disasters, active shooters, fire incidents, and multiple accident scenarios, among others.

One drill routinely performed in hospitals with pediatric and obstetric units is known as Code Pink. This drill aims to prevent the abduction of a child or infant from the hospital premises. When a Code Pink is announced over the speaker system, every hospital employee is assigned a specific task, such as guarding a front door, monitoring a side entrance, searching a floor, or overseeing a stairwell.

We have run drills where we actually bring in a person from outside and give them a doll, which is used to recreate the scene of a baby being stolen, and the staff attempts to stop them from exiting the facility.

While serving as the CEO of a hospital, I underwent ankle surgery and had a boot on my leg, which considerably slowed down my mobility.

One afternoon, while I was speaking with our Chief Nursing Officer, a Code Pink was initiated within the hospital. As the CEO, I was always aware of the drills scheduled to take place, and this was not one of them.

Hearing the code, the Chief Nursing Officer leaped from my office, heading to the area where the code was called: the second floor. I followed as fast I could, hobbling along.

When I finally managed to get to the second floor, the sight I saw there could have easily qualified for reality television. The security guard was sprawled across the floor, being attended to by a nurse. Our Chief Nursing Officer, who, by the way, was very well-trained in self-defense and de-escalation of situations, had a very large woman dressed as a nurse, restrained in an arm bar, holding her to the floor.

In another part of the area, two nurses had just pulled a baby out of a large shopping bag. Soon, the police arrived, and the woman who attempted to steal the infant was arrested. The security guard was visibly shaken but unharmed.

Our processes worked just as they should have. But for the first time since my surgery, I was happy my foot was in a cast, and I had to wear a boot, so I wasn't the first one on the scene with this very large and very aggressive kidnapper that my martial arts-trained Chief Nursing Officer was able to subdue!

The Fitness Center

During my career, I was a planner and a Vice President for new services. One of the projects I was involved with was a medical mall. The medical mall consisted of a fitness center, a joint venture surgery center, retail space, a large, upscale child enrichment center, and a large tennis center. The construction project was a tremendous learning experience for me, with numerous issues arising. I will share some of those way too exciting experiences with you.

The Hot Tub Encounter

The very first issue that arose was that we had opened the facility to members despite it not being totally completed. Construction final projects were taking a lot longer to be finished than they should have.

So, one evening, the General Manager and I decided to go to the center at night after we closed, and the contractors were supposed to be working on plumbing issues. But when we walked in, what we found was not at all what was expected.

Loud music was blaring in the $10 million fitness center. I couldn't see anyone working, so we kept looking, and eventually, we found the workers. The sight was borderline pornographic and laughable at the same time. Four workers were completely naked in the women's whirlpool, drinking beer.

Fortunately, I was able to hold back the General Manager, who wanted to do more than throw the workers out, and we left without incident. In the next few days, new workers arrived to complete the work without any more naked incidents!

Tile Troubles

One day, we noticed a yellowing of the drywall in a corridor outside the men's shower area. I asked the contractor what could be causing this discoloration. He said he thought it was temporary condensation that would stop. He suggested simply painting over the yellowing, which I firmly rejected as an unacceptable solution.

So again, two nights later, the general manager and I made another midnight visit. The general manager was well versed in plumbing, and given previous experience with the contractor, he was afraid that the copper pans that were to be installed under each shower stall to prevent leaking were not in place. We took a hammer and smashed the tiles in one of the individual shower stalls. And when we did, we discovered that there were no copper pans in that stall, nor were there any copper pans anywhere else.

So, we had to call the contractors back and have them install 12 copper pans in the men's showers, as well as 12 copper pans in the women's showers, to prevent further leaks. Under various threats, we received significant compensation back from the contractor for this scam.

Chasing Sprinklers

The day we were going to open the fitness center, we had a radio remote on air live in the lobby. I always had concerns about a sprinkler head that was installed in the steam room.

"Why in the world is there a sprinkler head in the steam room where we know it is going to be hot and probably set off the sprinkler, and there is nothing flammable in the steam room anyway?" I had asked the contractor.

But the contractor brushed my concerns off, saying "it was code" to have a sprinkler there and that it would not be a problem since the fuse in the sprinkler was designed such that it would not go off unless there was a fire. As you can probably guess, that was not what happened.

While the radio remote had just started, an alarm went off that the sprinkler in the steam room had gone off. *Wonderful.*

I saw the contractor running down the hallway. Up to this point, I had never seen him move faster than a southern crawl of a walk. So, I chased after him and asked what was going on. And he very urgently explained to me that if we didn't shut off the water supply within two minutes, every sprinkler in the building was going to go off. So, I found a comfortable chair, assessed my next job opportunities, and watched the sprinkler head in the ceiling over my head, waiting for it to begin to spew water.

Fortunately, I stayed dry and was able to prevent a disastrous situation.

The Key and the Handcuffs

As you can tell, the day of the opening was one worth remembering for all the wrong reasons. If the sprinkler incident wasn't enough, another memorable event took place the same day.

The fire marshal, who was supposed to carry out an inspection weeks before the opening, showed up on our opening day. He asked to visit certain areas of the facility; his last request was to see a specific closet that contained several electrical breakers.

While giving him the tour, I realized I didn't have the key to that closet and told him so. That didn't go too well, and I realized I was dealing with an egomaniac.

He moved his jacket to the side, showed me a pair of handcuffs, and said, "If you don't get me the key to that room in five minutes, I'm going to arrest you and shut down this facility for operating illegally without an approved fire inspection." I found the key, opened the room, did not assault the Fire Marshall, and was not arrested. We passed the inspection.

One evening, the Fire Department arrived at the fitness center because an alarm had sounded. The fire department's major problem was that no one could find the source of the fire, yet, strangely enough, there was a smell of smoke coming from the gym. The firefighters were about 2 minutes from putting axes into the walls to locate the source of the smoke.

Luckily, one of the firemen stepped outside and saw that a smoldering cigarette had been put in the mulch under an intake valve near our gym, which was causing the smoke to enter the gym, and there was no fire. Safe to say, it was just a blood pressure-raising false alarm.

Fitness, Faith, and Alcohol

Under immense pressure to make the fitness center financially viable, I made what some thought was a controversial decision. Despite being a health-oriented facility with a religious affiliation, I pursued a liquor license in my name. I got the license (proving to my wife I was not a felon!)

The goal was to serve beer and wine coolers in the café within the fitness center, taking advantage of the exorbitant 300% markup on alcohol. We installed 4 televisions in the fitness center that we kept tuned to sports. This took place 35 years ago, so I claim the invention of the sports bar.

 The introduction of beer and wine was a small part of profitability but was very successful in our membership retention, securing the future of the fitness center.

Cardiac Chaos

During the first week of our facility's opening, a film crew arrived early one morning to film an advertisement for us. To this point, not much had gone as planned with the opening, so why would this be different....

While the crew was setting up in the equipment area, a gentleman working out on a stepper suddenly experienced a cardiac event. Fortunately, he was given the required medical aid in time and, after a short hospital stay, went home.

It is poor form, but this "event" turned out to be a positive for us. The story that came out in the news broadcast on that television station was as follows:

 "This facility is a great place to have a heart attack if you're going to have one because physicians from the medical office building next door are always working out in the fitness center."

There was just one thing; the story missed the fact that the two physicians present on site were a psychiatrist and a dermatologist. In fact, the person who actually intervened, giving the person having the cardiac issue assistance, turned out to be a nurse who happened to be working out at the facility that day.

My last comment on the fitness center experience is the pressure that my boss, not a believer in the project, put on me. The week before opening, with a rather grim tone, he informed me that if the center didn't start generating positive cash flow within six months, I would not only be fired but also find myself buried in a shallow grave in a nearby rural county. And if you knew him, you too would question if it was a joke!

Unexpected Awards: Punched in the Nose

As healthcare leaders, we always prepare our teams for situations involving potential violence in the workplace. But I don't think we are ever actually prepared for every situation that could happen. At least I wasn't prepared for the situation that I'm about to unfold.

The emergency department, one of the most stressful areas in the hospital, can sometimes bring some very unexpected situations. In this particular case, I took on a temporary role at a large hospital, filling in for another administrator. The hospital had a busy emergency department and was located in a rough neighborhood. Instead of security officers, we had off-duty and armed police officers stationed in the emergency department.

On my third day at the hospital, I received a call from the corporate office requesting that I terminate the contract and remove from the hospital a physician working in the emergency department. I was told by corporate leadership that the physician was actually prescribing drugs not approved for use in the United States.

I walked to the emergency department and asked the physician in question to meet me in the break room. Seeking privacy, I closed the door and terminated the physician's contract, instructing him to leave immediately. He screamed at me as I left the room.

 I headed back to the nurse's station to get the guards to escort him from the premises. At the station, there were at least three nurses, another physician, and various hospital employees diligently performing their duties, but no security guards. Suddenly, the physician I had just terminated burst out of the breakroom and charged at me, and I believe his exact words were, "I'm going to beat the f-ing sh-t out of you!."

I put my hands up and said, "Wait a minute." But it was already too late. Just as the words left my mouth, he punched me square in the nose right between my outstretched hands. The impact threw me back against the nurse's station, and I could see he was preparing to hit me again. In self-defense, I raised my elbow, moved toward him, and struck him on the jaw as he approached. He fell to the floor, unconscious.

The staff quickly revived him and determined that he had a broken jaw. I ordered him to be handcuffed and transported by ambulance to another facility for treatment.

Several weeks later, I received notice that I was being sued by this disgruntled physician. However, the case was dropped within two months. But the story doesn't end there; here comes the best part.

During our annual meeting of all hospitals within the system, an award ceremony took place at the end of the event. Traditionally, these awards were given to hospital CEOs who had made significant contributions, such as initiating new programs, developing new facilities, improving the bottom line, or achieving exceptional quality levels.

Each CEO that was being given an award was called up on the stage with their picture being displayed on the Jumbo TV, and they were given a financial bonus for their achievements.

To my surprise, the very last picture to be displayed for an award was mine. I had no idea this was going to happen, as each previous award winner had made significant and noteworthy contributions to the organization.

Well, the bonus that I was given was for, let's say, "a unique achievement." My story, which I had been trying to keep as quiet as possible, was out in the open. The caption under my name read:

"Hard-Ass of the Year"

19

Winning the Lottery – Twice

I don't consider myself a big lottery player, only indulging a few times a year by buying a lottery ticket. On one rare occasion, however, I did manage to win $20. But that's another story.

While working at a hospital in the Southwest, I experienced a disturbing situation when my administrative assistant didn't show up to work without any prior notice or phone call, and we were unable to contact her. Naturally, we were all very worried about her whereabouts and safety. Four days later, we received a call from the FBI assuring us that she was safe and there was nothing to worry about. We knew her husband was an FBI agent, but we still worried. One week later, she contacted us herself, only to announce that she and her husband had won $14.8 million in the lottery and had gone "undercover."

 Several years later, my fiancé, now my wife of 30 years, Carrie, and I eloped to Tucson, where my multimillion-dollar winning assistant and FBI agent husband stood up for us as witnesses at our wedding.

At another hospital, we were preparing for a visit from the Joint Commission on Accreditation for Hospitals, who were scheduled to conduct a three-day survey at our facility. All members of leadership and key personnel involved in the survey had agreed to meet at 6 AM to ensure we had all necessary documents in order.

Around 7 AM, my administrative assistant, who was never late, entered the room, looking as if she had been mugged in the parking lot. Naturally concerned, I asked her if she was okay and what had happened. She then informed me that she and her husband had won $6.8 million in the lottery the previous night. Being slow, I questioned her again, to which she reiterated that they had indeed won $6.8 million in the lottery. I wanted to ask her a third time, but it finally sunk in!

She then proceeded to tell me and other employees in the room how much she loved working with us and was going to continue working at the hospital. We all had a good laugh at that!

Two weeks later, she handed in her resignation, and the last we heard, she and her husband were on a cruise in the South Pacific.

Foam Fiasco: A Birth Control Disaster

Early in my career, I had roles as a health and patient educator. In my undergraduate degree in Community Health Education, I had various courses focusing on drug and alcohol education, sex education, emotional and mental health, and more.

At one point, I volunteered at a family planning agency that provided contraception to those who could not afford it. My role as a male volunteer was to greet and thank the men who accompanied their spouses or girlfriends to the center, encouraging them to be supportive partners. I would also provide information on different contraceptive methods and discuss potential side effects.

One evening, while I was in the area designated for men, the physician came to me and said, "The female educator isn't here today. Would you mind going through different birth control methods with a group of young women? There are about 8 or 9 of them." I mistakenly, as it turns out, agreed.

I entered the room and asked the group what they were there for. They all raised their hands, saying that they wanted to get the pill.

Before they saw the doctor, I decided to explain what the pill does, its potential side effects, and other birth control options that they might consider in the future. I went through several methods, saving the demonstration of a foam contraceptive for last. This foam was dispensed from a pressurized container into an applicator and contained spermicide to prevent conception.

I thought it would be helpful to actually show how this worked, so I took the applicator in one hand and held it up so all could see me fill the applicator and then put the pressurized container up against the applicator to fill the applicator with the foam. As I did so, it slipped, and the spermicide shot in both of my eyes.

I could not see through the burning feeling in my eyes. The physician quickly came to my aid, rinsing my eyes with water. After about 30 minutes, I could see just fine through my bloodshot eyes.

Beyond the pain and embarrassment, I will never forget the girls' hysterical laughter as I left the room, with one girl managing to blurt out between laughs, "Oh yeah, forget the pill; give me that foam gun."

Foot-in-Mouth: I Didn't Hear That

Early in my career, when I was in my early 20s, I worked as a health planner for a small health system in the South. With a strong desire to impress my superiors and advance within the organization, I made it a habit to arrive at work early, usually between 6:30 AM and 7:00 AM, well ahead of the rest of the administration, who would arrive at 8:30 AM. The only other early riser was the Executive Assistant for the administration, a sweet southern lady in her mid to late 60s.

One morning, as I sat in my storage room office between the copy machine and fax machine, I overheard a page requesting a specific physician to contact the emergency department. It soon became apparent that the operator had forgotten to turn off her microphone, allowing us to listen in on her conversation with the other operator. The operators' and greeter's workspace was located in a glassed-in area in the main lobby of the large hospital. The conversation continued for a minute or two until I heard one of the operators exclaim while looking out at the lobby, "Look at that woman's britches! They're so big; she could fit a family full of (racist comment) in there."

Stunned, I stopped writing, frozen in place, and stared at the wall in front of me. Suddenly, the Executive Assistant rushed into my small area, her face filled with terror. Almost simultaneously, we both asked, "Did you hear that?" Realizing that we needed to take action, she declared, "We've got to do something."

Being in my early 20s and probably the lowest person on the totem pole in the organization's administration, I wasn't sure what to do next, although I had been involved with other human resources situations and knew that waiting another 2 hours until Senior Leaders arrived to take action regarding this was too long.

I decided to take the stairs six floors to the lobby to get there faster. I confronted the operator who had made the inappropriate comment, which was heard in almost 1,000,000 ft^2 of the very large hospital complex. I told her that she needed to go home and that human resources would contact her.

She balked at me initially until one of our physicians who had heard the inappropriate comment entered the conversation and backed me up on my demand. The operator went home, and, of course, she was subsequently terminated.

From Wisdom Teeth to A Bloody Shirt: A Dental Misadventure

Early in my career, I worked at a large clinic and hospital with a medical education program. At the time, I was in my early 20s and was informed that I needed to have all four of my wisdom teeth extracted. Being young and still unfamiliar with the intricacies of the medical field, I made the decision to approach the head of the oral surgery program to perform the procedure. I met with the physician, who immediately agreed to perform the surgery, stating that I should be glad he was the one performing the surgery and this would allow him to "keep his skills fresh."

Following the surgery, I returned to my duplex and dozed off on the couch. When I woke up, I jumped off the couch when I realized the front of my shirt was literally soaked in blood. I spent around 45 minutes attempting to stop the bleeding, but my efforts only slowed the process. So, I walked three blocks to the hospital, and since this was a large teaching program, I was seen by an oral surgery resident.

As the resident examined my mouth, he exclaimed, "Who butchered your mouth?" When I responded that it was Dr. X who had performed the surgery, the resident's candid reply was, "I didn't know that old fool still did surgeries."

So, the takeaway from this very traumatizing experience was a very valuable lesson—an attempt to receive care from a healthcare professional who regularly and consistently practices a specific procedure rather than solely relying on an academic who may not have regular hands-on experience.

Negotiations: Win-Win with the Union

At a very large hospital, as the President, I dealt daily with a very assertive union. All employees except management and food service workers were part of the union. Food service was not included in the union as it was a contract service with a well-known hotel organization.

This union had been in place for over 30 years and had clauses in its contract that had become untenable given the new financial constraints imposed on the hospital, including lower reimbursement and other challenges from the federal government and payers. Some employees were making more than 2 times more than their peers in other facilities in the market. Changing this would mean dramatic lifestyle changes for those involved.

I wanted to change the work rules, but I knew that achieving this would be nearly impossible outside of or even within union negotiations. The business agent for the union constantly pushed me to get rid of the hotel organization and make our 12-13 food service workers eligible for union membership. I negotiated with him for 2 months. He agreed to change three work rules in exchange for me terminating the hotel organization's contract and hiring those employees to work directly for us, thus making them union-eligible.

Adding these 12-13 employees to the existing 375 union workers was not an issue for me, but the work rule changes saved our hospital $3.2 million in the first year. The union official seemed more concerned about the number of employees in his portfolio rather than the well-being of his people, who had to make significant lifestyle changes after the changes took effect.

In the same hospital, which was part of a small health system, we had a successful year and decided to give every employee a small raise midyear, including at the union hospital where I worked.

However, the union accused us of trying to break their unity and cause dissent among the union members (probably true) and threatened legal action. They also placed 55-gallon drums around the hospital perimeter and encouraged employees to discard any items with the hospital's name, including sweatshirts, hats, key chains, t-shirts, and other materials we had previously provided, into these drums, stating that they wanted a decent raise instead. They even threatened a strike, which never happened.

Today, the union in this hospital is decertified. During my time there, the union's newsletter (during negotiations) depicted a caricature of me walking the plank on a pirate ship with a sword in my back.

Anesthesia Antics: There's Nothing Like Being Sued

In a large hospital in the Midwest, we identified that the quality of our anesthesia services was hindering our ability to attract surgeons from the community. So, we decided to cancel the existing anesthesia contract, providing the contracted group with the required six months' notice as stated in the agreement.

We initiated the process of interviewing new groups to take over the anesthesia practice at our hospital once the existing contract expired.

A physician leader involved with the interview process of new groups made a comment to one of the groups we were interviewing, saying, "We need to get rid of the old (he used a slur to identify the group)." The anesthesiologists in this group were primarily of one "ethnicity."

Word of this got back to the group we were terminating, and they sued our health system, hospital, me included, for several million dollars.

My role in this process was to ensure, through deposition, that the decision to hire a new anesthesia group was not influenced by this physician or by my superiors at the corporate office. Instead, it was solely based on the merits of selecting a high-quality anesthesia provider.

One advantage I had in defending against the lawsuit was that a member of the ethnic group in question had actually played a role in raising me after my father passed away when I was 15. This personal connection clearly demonstrated that there was no bias on my part during the decision-making process, which was genuinely focused on selecting the best provider based on their qualifications. As a result, the lawsuit was dropped, and

we terminated the physician who made these inappropriate
comments from our organization.

From Hawaii to Florida: There's No Place to Hide

Early in my career, I applied for a job at a rehabilitation hospital in Hawaii. I was flown to Hawaii for an intense three days of interviews.

The last part of my interview was to give a talk to approximately 80 employees of the hospital. I was asked to speak about the differences between for-profit and not-for-profit hospitals, in my opinion.

I gave what I thought was a solid explanation, gathered my things, and headed for the airport. Many hours later, I arrived back home in Florida. I decided that the pay structure and island lifestyle were not for me.

Three weeks later, I decided to check on the progress of some renovations underway in the physical therapy department. As I walked in, the director introduced me to a traveling/contract physical therapist who would be with us for the next three months.

The physical therapist greeted me with an odd smile on his face. He took me aside and said, "I was in the audience three weeks ago in Hawaii when you gave your talk about for-profit versus not-for-profit hospitals." It was his last day as a contract therapist in Hawaii!

Since my current employer did not know that I was interviewing for other jobs, I was glad to hear him say, "You were never there."

As they say, there's no place to hide.

The Turkey: A Thanksgiving Tale

Cost controls and efficiencies are critical factors for hospital success in providing cost-effective, quality care to patients. During a period of financial strain, non-essential expenses must be cut or postponed.

In early November, I took on the temporary role of CEO at a struggling rehabilitation hospital, tasked with implementing a turnaround plan to ensure its viability. This particular hospital had a tradition of giving each employee the gift of a 12-to-15-pound turkey for Thanksgiving. When it came to cuts in expenses, eliminating this perk, I decided it would be one of the most innocuous and painless approaches on my list of cuts.

While some understood the reasoning behind it and knew the alternatives, others did not.

One morning, I arrived at the hospital only to find a large cardboard turkey, which was a holiday decoration on the lobby wall, with its head replaced by a picture of my own.

Though tempted to make a joke about "rolling heads," I decided against it.

An Unexpected Connection: The Hotline

To ensure that employees are comfortable sharing their ethical concerns without fear of repercussions or retaliation, many hospitals have an ethics hotline. These hotlines are meant to give employees confidence that someone safe, higher up in the organization, will listen to their concerns, and any offender will be held responsible.

One afternoon, I received a call from our ethics hotline. The situation relayed to me was that a student nurse had called the hotline, fearing that our dialysis equipment was killing patients. I immediately investigated and brought in physicians, nurses, and technicians to evaluate the equipment and overall situation.

It turned out that two patients had died not very long after receiving dialysis. However, it was found that one of the patients was a terminal AIDS patient and died of other causes. The second death was of a 97-year-old woman, who the medical staff determined her death was due to other causes as well.

An interesting outcome of this situation was that when I got back to the hotline representative who was on the other side of the country from me; I was in Florida, and she was in California, I learned something interesting.

We learned that we were both from Wisconsin and grew up within 20 miles of each other. Her father had been a primary care physician who also did obstetrics in a small hospital near my hometown. After learning this information, I went home and looked at my birth certificate, and I was able to connect the dots. Her father was the physician in attendance at my birth.

The Bribe: Corruption in a Hospital

Many things need to be worked out when opening a new hospital. Equipment needs to be tested, and policies and procedures need to be put in place, validated, and become part of the culture. There is much training that needs to be accomplished with employees and physicians. Vendors need to be assessed, hired, and evaluated.

When opening a hospital, you are literally hiring hundreds of people from all backgrounds and professions, from housekeepers and technicians to professionals and medical staff. During such circumstances, you're often forced to rely on references, which can often be unreliable.

One of the primary examples of a bad hire occurred in a new hospital where I was the Executive Vice President of the 4 hospital Region.

One morning, the CEO called me, asking to speak with me in person. So, I drove to the hospital, which was two hours away. When I got there, he was in his office alongside a radiology tech. The radiology tech stated that a radiologist had offered to pay him to erase a series of scans.

For a good minute or two, I just stared at him in disbelief. Finally, coming out of my shock, we decided to handle things subtly and asked the tech to remain quiet as we conducted the investigation.

After contacting the police and working with their detectives, we decided to place a recording device on the tech the next time he interacted with the radiologist in question (with his consent, of course).

Indeed, even during the second interaction, the radiologist blatantly offered the tech a significant amount of money to erase six scan screenings. After some research, it was determined that the physician had missed several obvious cancerous lumps from a series of CAT scans. The scans in question were 6 months old. He knew that other radiologists who viewed new scans recently taken and made comparisons would see that he had missed the obvious tumors. These tumors had grown in size over the 6-month period.

The physician was summarily terminated from our medical staff immediately. He was arrested the same day and was subsequently convicted of the crime.

Tragic Departure: Truly a Sad Ending

After having coffee in the cafeteria with one of the oncologists in a large hospital, we headed to the oncology department on the fifth floor. Since we were both runners, we decided to take the stairs. As we stepped onto the landing of the fourth floor, we heard a loud noise, which I knew after 30 years of hunting and shooting could only be a gunshot.

It came from above us, so (for some crazy reason) we climbed onto the next flight as fast as possible and opened the door to the fifth floor to see if the gunshot had come from there.

What we saw was a horrific scene that I will never forget. There was the body of a man who had shot himself in the head to commit suicide. He had previously been a patient in the oncology unit.

Afterward, it was determined that though his cancer was in remission, other issues in his personal life had thrown him into a deep depression.

In his very confused mind, he wanted to die near the people that he cared about the most, the people in the oncology unit that he felt had saved his life, as bizarre as that sounds.

Though the team in the oncology unit often dealt with death, the violent gunshot suicide caused several employees to resign, and others had to go through extensive counseling.

Working in a warm climate and tourist area can be a challenge, especially when you must staff a hospital. The census or number of patients visiting and being admitted to the hospital can change dramatically based on the season.

One hospital where I worked had many so-called snowbirds in wintertime who lived in the area six months of the year in the winter and returned to the Northern parts of the United States to enjoy the summer months.

Staffing the hospital during these months when the volume was high, sometimes 40% higher in winter than in the summertime, was a great challenge.

Our human resources director was from London, England. Through her connections, she was able to get us four to five intensive care nurses each winter season. These nurses were of great help to us and were always very excited to leave dreary, cold old London for the warmer climate of our resort area hospital.

These intensive care nurses were very traditional; some even still wore their nursing hats. They were very skilled and very respectful to the physicians, even jumping from their chairs and offering the chairs to the doctors when they entered the room. The Physicians appreciated these nurses for their skills and deference to the point where when they would return to London, physicians had a going away party which, to some degree, I kid you not, resembled a funeral. The physician's depression lasted for weeks….

Bear in a Compactor: Rural Animal Excitement

After working for a while in a rural hospital in a mountainous area, it was not uncommon to see deer, elk, or even moose on hospital property. But what would get our attention most often was when we would see bears.

Incidents of bears breaking into cars in our parking lot or trying to enter our kitchen at night were not rare occurrences. We constantly had to remind our out-of-state visitors and patients that these bears were not pets, even though the locals knew them by name!

One of the strangest bear incidents I can recall is when one of the bears was stuck in a garbage compactor outside the emergency entrance to the hospital.

Animal control was able to extract the bear, but it was a two-hour extravaganza for employees and patients to watch from afar.

Police Protection: A Rehab Hospital's Security Dilemma

When leading a large 80-bed rehabilitation hospital, I was approached to meet with the County Sheriff and the magistrate or judge.

The meeting was to inform me that a convicted murderer who was serving time in our county prison for murder had contracted Guillain-Barre syndrome. They wanted to admit this patient to the hospital for therapy. Everything seemed "pretty normal" until they told me the patient would have an armed guard with him 24/7.

If you are familiar with Guillain-Barre syndrome, you know that most patients are basically paralyzed, cannot move their limbs, and need assistance with all daily activities. My point to the sheriff and magistrate was that we really didn't need an armed guard and that our staff could handle any situation that came up with this patient.

That was when I was informed that the armed guard was not to protect us against the patient but to protect the patient from the family members of the murder victim. These family members had sworn revenge and promised publicly to kill this patient at any opportunity they got.

This led to a very detailed conversation where we discussed the circumstances of external security, police surveillance, and just when a gun could be fired in our hospital. Fortunately, the patient fully recovered within six days and was able to return to prison without incident.

Spirited Meetings: Pass Me a Beer

About 30 years ago, I was the CEO of a hospital that was 40% owned by a group of physicians. I attended all medical staff leadership meetings held in the evenings in our hospital conference room. There were 2 meetings each month.

Besides doing a presentation on hospital operations, quality, safety, and strategy and answering questions, one of my responsibilities, though bartending was not covered in any of my degree programs for the meeting, was to unlock and roll the liquor cabinet to the meeting room from its storage area in administration.

Obviously, having liquor served at the meeting was not helpful to the discussions or outcomes of the meeting.

So, I decided to work with the corporate office to end the serving of alcohol at our staff meetings. We quoted nonexistent policies and covenants prohibiting alcohol, and after some time, it worked.

Besides getting some actual, sober work done at the meetings, one of the upsides of this change for me was that the meeting time was cut by over an hour to an hour and a half.

I was the new CEO of a small hospital in Florida when, on my third day of work, a detective barged into my office, pushing past my assistant, insisting that he had to speak with me. He claimed to have been working with the previous CEO, investigating a theft at our hospital, for over three months.

He told me he had agents from his firm coming into our hospital dressed in Federal Express and UPS uniforms and following the employee in question home at night. The video evidence that he showed me validated that one of my managers had been stealing large quantities of equipment and materials to build a cabin.

Some of the equipment stolen included pipes, electrical materials, 2x4s, bathtubs, paneling, sinks, and roofing materials, to name a few of the items.

I called our corporate office for directions since I was new to this facility and was instructed to terminate this employee immediately.

I remembered the employee in question was a very large, intimidating individual. I went through his resume and found that he had been in the military, where he was responsible for demolition and explosives. *This isn't scary at all,* I thought to myself.

So, because of this employee's military background, the corporate office actually sent an armed guard to be in the office next to me in case something should occur when I broke the news of his termination. I expected the worst.

As I laid out the charges for him and discussed the possible jail time, which could have been up to 10 years, much to my surprise, he began crying and apologizing.

So, the situation was handled, and he was terminated without incident. Most of the stolen materials were recovered, and the corporate office dealt with potential charges.

Afterward, this situation turned into a standing joke with the hospital managers. At the end of each managers' meeting, the managers thought they were really funny, drawing cards to see who would start my car in case there was a bomb attached to the ignition.

Memory Marvels: Meeting a Legend

As a new hospital CEO, there are many things that you must learn quickly. One of the facilities that I was new to was constructing a medical office building next to the hospital. I asked who the developer was and was told it was a company out of Birmingham, Alabama, called Starr/Sanders. Being from Wisconsin, I asked myself the question, *Birmingham/Starr?*

Bart Starr, the longtime quarterback of my favorite football team, the Green Bay Packers, went to college in Alabama. I wanted to confirm if it was his company.

I found out it was indeed Bart Starr's company as he arrived two days later for a meeting with physicians and to tour the new medical office building in an attempt to sell the condominium spaces to physicians.

My interaction with Mr. Starr was incredibly limited. I had a brief introduction as the new CEO. The following day, about 10 of us from the hospital had lunch with Mr. Starr. I felt sorry for the man as he could barely eat his lunch as people kept coming up to our table asking for his autograph. And again, my interaction with him was no more, no less than the other nine people at the table.

About three months later, I was at an airport in Cincinnati, talking with an old friend, when I felt a large hand on my shoulder. I turned around to see Bart Starr.

"Dan, how are you doing? And how's the project moving forward?" He spoke with a friendly smile. Now again, I had incredibly limited interaction with Mr. Starr.

I laughed to myself about his amazing memory. Knowing that I would be lucky to remember where I parked my car when I returned to the airport.

Pain, Paws, and Laughter: Anything for a Man's Best Friend

While leading an orthopedic rehabilitation hospital, I joined the hospital's volleyball team.

During a game, when spiking the volleyball, I felt a sharp pain in the back of my leg. The pain was bad but tolerable. The next day, I went to work, but the pain was getting worse, so I visited an orthopedic surgeon who was also playing on our team the night before. After looking at my leg, he looked at me and said, "You should not be walking. Your Achilles tendon is completely severed."

I underwent surgery two days later. I took one day to recover at home and went back to work. On my first day coming home from work, I was coming up the steps to my house on crutches. As I opened the door, the first thing I saw was my Labrador Retriever lying upside down. The scene almost made my heart stop because she didn't look like she was breathing.

I laid my crutches down and quickly crawled over to her. Thankfully, I could feel her shallow breathing. Looking to my left, I found an empty bottle of my pain medicine, which had been full, all chewed up, with no pills left in it.

I crawled to my phone and called the veterinarian, who gave me instructions on how to get the dog to vomit and keep her hydrated. After close to 90 minutes, she started to come back to life.

At this point, I hadn't had any pain meds for 10 hours. I started having some serious pain in my leg. On top of that, I had been crawling on the floor for over an hour. So, I decided to call my orthopedic surgeon and teammate. As I relayed the situation and my need for additional narcotics for pain, he began to laugh so hard that I had to hold the phone away from my ear.

"I've heard of dogs eating homework but never eating someone's narcotics," he managed to say between laughs. Thankfully, after he was done with the jokes, he was able to help me with a call to the pharmacy, assuring them that my return for more pain medication was not drug abuse but was legit!

A Colorful Conundrum in the Emergency Room: Joe, Joe, and Joe

As the CEO of a large hospital, I would often make rounds in different areas and departments. One morning, while talking with team members in the emergency department, I overheard a conversation that there was some confusion about patient names.

This emergency department was quite large, with 16 individual treatment areas. The confusion, as it turns out, was the fact that there were three "Joes" with the exact same last name in our emergency department at the same time.

The team came up with a fantastic idea of keeping them separate. They became Joe Green, Joe Red, and Joe Yellow.

All 3 were treated, released, or admitted without any name confusion.

Slopes, Shingles, and Smoke: Is the Hospital on Fire?

In my career, I have worked at many hospitals, including some that were quite old. One particular hospital stood out as it was nearly 80 years old.

The fifth floor of the hospital had such a significant slope that nurses had to lock the wheels of the gurneys to prevent them from rolling backward. Adding to its antiquity, the emergency phone in the elevator was a rotary phone.

Due to its age, this hospital was not originally designed for helicopter transfers, so nearby homes and parking lots were built in close proximity. During our first helicopter arrival, we had to clear the parking area, and the strong rotor wash actually blew shingles off the roofs of two houses.

Given budget constraints, the hospital had been making do with an old emergency generator. Although it emitted a distinct smell and smoke, with the help of some duct tape and glue, the maintenance team managed to keep it functioning.

One afternoon, I heard sirens and saw the fire department pulling into our parking lot. I knew we had been performing a routine test of our old emergency generator that produces smoke. Seeing the smoke, one of the neighbors called the fire department, saying that the hospital was on fire!

If there was an upside, it was that the incident convinced our corporate leadership to get us a new emergency generator.

Happy Hour: Innocent Rattlesnakes

Working in a hospital in the desert presents unique challenges that are not commonly encountered in urban facilities.

Dehydration, falls from hiking, overheating, bites of all types, and extreme sunburn are just a few examples. One unexpected scenario we frequently encountered in our emergency department was rattlesnake bites. On average, in the busy season, we dealt with one to two snake bite cases per week. A major issue we faced was the high cost of antivenom for these bites, which often were given to people who could not pay or weren't covered by insurance.

In order to better understand the situation, our physicians conducted an informal assessment over a period of three months. Surprisingly, they concluded that over 50% of the snakebite cases involved alcohol. When I shared this finding with our Board of Directors, believe it or not, one board member asked where the snakes were getting into alcohol. We did not have IQ standards for board members.

Hospital Havoc: Hurricane Confusion

If there's an upside to hurricanes versus tornadoes, it's that you get a little more warning with hurricanes. As a hospital CEO in Florida, we received a warning that a hurricane was projected to hit us in about three days. The hospital was near the beach on a bay and only about 7 feet above sea level, so we immediately started taking aggressive measures. Our first priority was to transfer our remaining patients to other facilities and reinforce the hospital entrances with sandbags. Most of our expensive radiology and surgery equipment was located on the first floor.

Once all the patients had been safely relocated and the staff departed, I left to prepare my home for the impending hurricane. As I pulled into my driveway, I noticed my neighbor throwing his lawn furniture into his pool to prevent it from blowing away. I found that very resourceful.

Just as I was about to ask him about his strategy to keep items from blowing away, my phone rang—it was the Sheriff's Department. One of their officers had, against protocol and plan, begun to advise citizens who were unsure of where to seek shelter to come to the hospital after we had just evacuated. Without wasting any time, I quickly turned around and returned to the hospital, working closely with the Sheriff's Department to accommodate those in need and redirect others to alternative resources.

Fortunately, the worst of the hurricane ended up missing our area, and we only experienced heavy rains for a few hours.

The Clipboard Routine: Halftime Excitement

A hospital system I worked for constructed a large fitness center that housed a highly successful sports medicine program. This program collaborated with the women's athletic program at a major university, providing assistance with athletic and strength training. As a gesture of gratitude, the university extended an offer to my boss, the system President, to be a guest coach for an upcoming home women's basketball game against another nationally-ranked opponent. However, my boss declined the opportunity and offered it to me instead, and I eagerly accepted.

Being a guest coach entailed sitting at the end of the bench during the game and joining the coaches in the locker room during halftime to listen to their pep talk and discuss the second half's strategy. The head coach of the team was renowned for being one of the top-ranked coaches in the country. She had a reputation for being vocal, emotional, and direct during halftime.

At halftime, with the home team trailing by three points, the coach passionately delivered her speech, telling the team that they were too tight and letting this big game get to them mentally. In this moment of intense emotion, she threw her clipboard against the wall near my chair. Caught off guard, I tumbled off my chair and ended up flat on the floor, causing the entire women's team to burst into laughter. Apparently, the coach often resorted to throwing her clipboard, and the team was accustomed to it. However, I was unaware of this custom, which was why I was sprawled across the floor, unhurt but looking very silly.

The team went on to win the game by two points. I took full credit for the victory, as I believed that the team laughing at my fall helped relax them in the second half!

Unexpected Grievances: Fun with the Union

On my first day as the new administrator at a hospital in the Midwest, I was approached by hospital leadership and informed that I would be handling union grievances, specifically third-step grievances. Due to a four-month delay in getting a new administrator, there was an urgent third-step grievance from the union that needed immediate attention.

The situation involved a situation where a patient failed to show up for surgery, and an employee in the surgery department complained about a problem with her nose. In an impromptu decision, the ENT surgeon performed a procedure on the employee while she was under local anesthesia administered by the anesthesiologist. The previous administration had taken action against both the anesthesiologist and the surgeon, and the employee who underwent the procedure had been given a two-week suspension. The union was grieving this two-week punishment.

Initially, I believed this grievance was a prank being played on the new administrator, as the situation seemed too surreal to be true. However, I proceeded with the meeting, only to discover that it was indeed a legitimate grievance. After carefully considering the details, I threw out the grievance, and we moved forward.

Union relations within this health system were not good. Previously, the health system leader had made a comment that was overheard during union negotiations: "If the nurses need more money, let them find a rich guy to marry."

About a week after this comment was overheard, a dozen nurses showed up to picket our corporate office. What made this picketing unique was that the nurses were wearing wedding dresses and carrying signs that read "Marry Me." We actually made national news with this disaster.

Late one afternoon, I was in a bustling emergency department engaged in a conversation with one of the physicians on duty.

Suddenly, a loud commotion caught our attention, prompting us to turn and witness an individual brandishing a gun while demanding to know where a specific person was. Reacting swiftly, one of the other emergency room physicians and our security guard cautiously approached the individual and falsely informed him that the person he was looking for had already received treatment and been discharged, even though it was not true.

Actually, the person he was searching for was still being treated in one of our emergency department bays behind a curtain, being prepared for surgery. In response to this information, the gunman promptly fled the scene. Fortunately, he was apprehended within less than 30 minutes.

It was later discovered that he was the same person who had initially shot the patient in the leg and had come to our emergency department with the intention of "finishing the job."

Prescription Predicament: Falling Out of My Pocket

A human resources leader asked me to attend a meeting in her office along with an employee and a Deputy Sheriff. The purpose of the meeting was to address a concerning issue related to paper prescriptions from our emergency department that were surfacing at local pharmacies under dubious circumstances for controlled substances.

The physician's name on these prescriptions was just a scribble, and the drugs prescribed were narcotics. It was suspected that a single individual was responsible for this misuse of paper prescriptions.

During the meeting, the human resources director skillfully managed to get the employee to admit that he had "inadvertently" placed some prescription pads in his pocket during work and had forgotten to take them out.

According to him, these pads might have fallen out while he was reaching into his pocket to retrieve his keys.

The sheriff questioned him, "How could something fall out of your pocket simply by putting your hands in and out of it?"

The not-so-bright employee demonstrated his explanation by reaching into his jacket pockets and pulling his hands back out. To my disbelief, along with his hand, emerged a sizable bag of marijuana, narrowly missing landing on the sheriff's foot. It was definitely a "did that just happen?" moment.

It is important to note that this incident took place nearly 30 years ago when having a large bag of marijuana in front of a sheriff's deputy was definitely not a good thing.

Expensive Lighting: A Costly Compromise

I was once part of a hospital located in an affluent area where we undertook a project to construct a much-needed parking garage. The garage was designed with two above-ground levels and one below-ground level.

Naturally, we ensured that the parking lot was well-lit during nighttime to prioritize the safety and security of our employees. However, one influential individual in the community would drive past our hospital on his way home in the dark and voiced a complaint. He claimed that the lights in the parking garage were too harsh on his eyes and affected his driving ability as he passed the garage. Rather than approaching me directly to discuss the matter, he took his concern directly to the City Council.

As a result, the City Council, giving into the political influences and pressures, compelled us to install sconces on the lights to reduce the lighting reaching the road's travel surface. Interestingly, no other frequent users of that busy road had ever complained about the lighting.

The cost of installing these sconces amounted to $148,000, not what I would call a good use of community resources.

When I was a young boy, I would accompany my father on Saturdays as he made stops and engaged in conversations with different people in our small community. During those times, my father would often share stories of his experiences as a military policeman (MP) in Korea during the Korean War. One particular story that he told involved him being assigned to be a bodyguard for General Douglas MacArthur.

In this story, my father recounted how General MacArthur was scheduled to address several hundred South Korean soldiers who were gathered on a hillside. The general approached the microphone and spoke for about a minute, sharing a joke. He then stepped back, and the interpreter took his turn at the microphone, speaking for only eight or nine seconds. To everyone's surprise, the entire hillside erupted in laughter. General MacArthur, infuriated, looked at the interpreter and hollered, "I took my time to tell that joke, and you spit it out in ten seconds? What did you say?" The interpreter calmly responded, "I told them to show the General respect; he told a funny joke. You all be polite, and all laugh."

This story will tie back to my healthcare experiences….Fast forward to the early days of my career as a new Vice President for a small hospital system, where I found myself struggling to balance multiple tasks and responsibilities across several hospitals. Recognizing my challenges, my boss, a great leader, approached me one morning and said, "You have worked at the Mayo Clinic; you have been in graduate school and have done internships. You need to toughen up and get into the real world and become more assertive and decisive."

To emphasize his point, he placed a biography of Douglas MacArthur on my desk and encouraged me to read it. As I delved into the book, halfway through, I stumbled upon the story my father had shared countless times during my childhood—a story that I had doubted. At this point, my father had been dead for ten years, and it was too late to verbally apologize to him, but I did so through prayer.

A Startling Incident: Do Not Move the Body

While working at a hospital in Florida, my wife and I had the pleasure of hosting my mother during her visit to see her new Granddaughter. We enjoyed our time together, and when the day came for her departure, we accompanied her to the airport to assist with check-in. However, just as we were about to bid her farewell, an urgent call interrupted our plans—a body had been discovered near one of the side doors of our hospital.

The police and County Medical Examiner were alerted to the situation. The ME required us to leave the body undisturbed until he arrived. The police had cordoned off the area with yellow caution tape, marking it as a restricted zone. It was nearly 98 degrees that day, and the body was lying on one of the pressure plates that opened the side door. Hot air was entering the hospital lobby, and it was getting very hot. The heat was not doing the body any good either.

The coroner finally arrived four hours later to examine the body. Initially, there were concerns that the body might belong to one of our hospital's employees, as they were found wearing a hospital scrub top.

However, after reviewing security cameras, it was found that four guys in a pickup truck drove to the side of the hospital, and instead of taking him to the emergency room, possibly out of fear of being reported, they threw the body out. The license plate was on our surveillance video, and they were later arrested.

The following day, upon arriving at the hospital, I discovered that my "hilarious" staff had sealed my office door with the very same yellow crime scene tape that had once marked the spot where the body had been found. Not a reminder I needed on a Monday morning.....

Diversity and Radioactivity: Tales from an East Tennessee Hospital

During my tenure as the President of a hospital in East Tennessee, I was part of a unique community—a place intertwined with nuclear history and technological advancements. This city, known for its contribution to the development of components for nuclear bombs in the 1940s, stands proud today with three operational nuclear plants and continuous breakthroughs in various technologies.

With 3 nuclear plants only a few miles from the hospital, we were sure that there were Russian subs off the North Carolina coast with us in the crosshairs.

Jokingly, I would often remark that our emergency department had no "normal" patients. This sentiment arose from the fact that our hospital catered to a diverse range of individuals.

Many residents from the hills of East Tennessee would arrive at our emergency department, having gone without medical care for years, presenting numerous comorbidities and serious health concerns. Alternatively, highly educated executives from the nuclear plants would visit the emergency department armed with web searches, eager to engage in extended discussions about their conditions with our emergency room doctors. It seemed that our medical staff was continuously navigating the contrasting needs of these two distinct patient populations.

The level of technical expertise among the nuclear plant staff was extraordinary. When a nuclear accident occurred in Japan, the husband of one of my employees was immediately flown in a jet, with midair refueling, to get his expert participation in containing the accident and controlling the nuclear fallout at the site as soon as possible.

One intriguing aspect of this area was its unique historical backdrop. The nuclear plants had been operating for nearly 60 years, with remnants of the past still visible throughout the city. Military-style numbered stoplights and barracks that once housed workers from the 1940s served as reminders of the area's nuclear heritage. Interestingly, as the hospital president, I did not have access to the hospital's basement, which was operated and staffed by individuals from the Department of Energy. Doing what I was not allowed to know!

Another notable occurrence within the vicinity of the nuclear plants was the rising number of deer-car collisions since the vast acreage had been closed to all but a few workers at the plants, and no public access was allowed. In fact, a small army guarded the area.

To address the deer-car issue, it was decided to open certain areas of the reservation surrounding the plants for archery deer hunting. Curiosity aroused, and as a history buff, I obtained an archery tag. I did more exploring than hunting and did not shoot a deer. Instead, I wanted to experience firsthand an area that had been restricted from general public access for over six decades. I saw unique radiation-checking devices, beautiful ponds, stunning geographic structures, and at least 40 very tame deer.

At the end of the day, I visited the checking station where hunters who had shot deer were required to register their harvested deer. There, I found two deer that were found to be radioactive. The game wardens, for safety reasons, prohibited the hunters from taking any part of the deer, including their antlers.

But we were told not to worry; everything is safe...

Crazy Termination: A CEO's Dilemma

During my time as the CEO of a Florida hospital, an employee believed she had been wronged by the facility. Despite her dissatisfaction, the employee did not wish to quit but rather sought to be terminated for her obvious desire to sue the organization. Although the employee consistently exhibited disruptive behavior, I was advised by our legal team not to terminate her.

One afternoon, the director of surgery rushed to my office, urging me to come down to the surgery area. The employee in question had urinated in her pants, walked all over the hospital, and was spreading the false narrative that her boss had denied her permission to use the restroom, forcing her to urinate on herself.

Familiar with her boss and aware that the story was fabricated, I promptly contacted our attorneys without seeking permission to terminate, instead informing them of my decision to dismiss the employee. I requested that they prepare the necessary termination documents.

As I proceeded with the termination, the employee handed me the documents outlining where to send her final paycheck and the contact information for her attorney, among other well-prepared details. She was gleefully prepared to be terminated. Subsequently, she filed a lawsuit against the hospital, leading to eight months of depositions and other proceedings. Eventually, the case was dropped.

Compromise Failure: A Lesson Learned

Early in my career, I was a leader of a team given the task of transforming an unused six-story nursing dormitory into a cancer center—a project that ultimately proved successful. However, towards the end of the project, an unexpected challenge emerged in the form of an underutilized swimming pool located in the basement of the building. As we worked on refurbishing the pool to make it functional again, I was approached by two groups expressing their desire to use it.

The first group was the hospital rehabilitation department, including inpatient rehabilitation, wishing to utilize the pool for patient therapy. Their goal was to conduct therapy sessions in the pool, requiring the water temperature to be at 96°. On the other hand, there was a group of employees who were avid lap swimmers seeking to use the pool for exercise. Naturally, they had their own temperature preference and wanted the water temperature closer to 78°.

Being young, inexperienced, and just plain dumb, I attempted to reach a compromise by setting the temperature at 85°. Now, anyone with common sense would know that this turned out to be a disaster. Both groups were upset with me for obvious reasons.

This experience taught me a valuable lesson about the importance of decisiveness. Later in my career, I had the opportunity to listen to Margaret Thatcher speak during a meeting in Arizona; her words resonated deeply with me. She declared that the most dangerous place on the highway of life is standing in the middle of the road where you are bound to get hit—a sentiment that aligned perfectly.

Costly Consequences: A Misguided CFO

When opening a hospital in the Southwest, I was asked by my boss to hire a friend of his who was an unemployed Chief Financial Officer (CFO). However, this individual had no prior hospital experience and very limited experience working in a larger organization. During the interview process, he appeared to be quite quirky. Despite my concerns and arguments with my boss about hiring someone more qualified, I was overruled, and we proceeded to open the hospital in July.

In January and February, when our employees began filing their income taxes, it came to light that our CFO had made changes to the withholding of many employees' taxes in an attempt to "help" them. Being a new facility, no one caught this.

Unfortunately, this action resulted in several dozen employees owing back taxes, and a few even incurred penalties. While our organization could pay the penalties, we couldn't cover the back taxes. As you can imagine, this was a nightmare as the leader responsible, particularly because a significant portion of our workforce lived paycheck to paycheck.

In a feeble attempt to mitigate the situation, we worked to set up payment plans and secure loans for the affected employees, offering them assistance in navigating through the tax repayment process. However, this incident tarnished our relationship with our employees and created a significant setback for our organization and personal threats to members of leadership. Overcoming the damage caused by this incident proved to be a difficult challenge.

I left as soon as I got my resume updated!

Hospital Transitions: Closing the Doors

Throughout my career, I have been involved in the opening of seven hospitals, encompassing acute care and rehabilitation facilities. I have also encountered the challenging task of closing three hospitals.

One of the hospitals I closed was very near another hospital within the same healthcare system. We conducted community meetings to discuss the reasoning behind the closure, which was pretty obvious but still emotional. The hospital only averaged 1-2 inpatient patients per week. After the closure, we planned to establish a large multispecialty clinic and an urgent care center, recruit physicians to the area, and develop a skilled nursing center—all essential services that the community required. Even still, the community did not receive the closure news well. To ensure that I made it out alive after some of the community meetings discussing closure, I made sure to have my Director of Development, who happened to be a former collegiate football player (6' 5", 250#), accompany me every time I exited the building!

The second closure I was involved in was a contract situation where I assisted a small struggling hospital in a joint venture with a larger health system. Unfortunately, due to some irregularities in one of the system hospitals located in another state, the joint venture was called off. Consequently, I was tasked with spending four months winding down and ultimately closing the hospital.

The third closure involved a very large hospital that was constructed in 1933 but had been surrounded by larger system-owned hospitals owned by well-known healthcare corporations. Eventually, this hospital was sold and transformed into condominiums.

Though these closures were difficult for all involved, I learned some valuable lessons during these closures. Many times, a lot more can be learned from challenging, troubled, and failed situations than we can learn from mountaintop successes.

Being Hacked and Held Hostage: Cyber Threats in Healthcare

In a small hospital where I served as CEO, we experienced a cyber-attack that resulted in a ransom demand for the unlocking of all our human resources records. The hacker demanded a $500,000 ransom in exchange for releasing the data back to us. Plus, they threatened to distribute personal details from the records all over the Internet. Swiftly, we engaged the FBI in the matter, and through their assistance, we were able to retrieve the data without succumbing to the ransom demands.

On another occasion, I received a call from one of my senior employees while she was at a grocery store purchasing ten $100 gift cards "for me." Our system's email had been hacked, and the perpetrator had contacted several of my directors in person, requesting them to buy the gift cards and scratch off the numbers on the back. They were then instructed to send the card numbers, as well as the numbers on the back of the cards after they had scratched them, to the address provided in the email. The fraudulent email claimed that the funds were needed for clients, even though, as a hospital administrator, I do not have clients. Fortunately, the employee making the purchase was informed by the cashier about similar hacking incidents, prompting her to contact me immediately. Consequently, I was able to intervene and halt the transaction. Funnily enough, ten minutes later, another employee was at the grocery store attempting to buy the same ten gift cards and comply with the instructions from the hacked email.

The bottom line of the incident revealed that I had some employees who were loyal to a fault and others who followed protocol and training when it came to suspicious e-mails.

Despite our efforts to implement software updates and conduct educational sessions cautioning against opening unknown emails or attachments, the fact remains that hackers possess the ability to breach even the most secure systems. If they can hack into the Pentagon, hacking into a 25-bed hospital could be done in their sleep.

Assessments and Assumptions: Aerobics Must Be the Answer

During my time in graduate school, I accepted an internship to conduct an assessment in the safety department of a large air conditioning and furnace manufacturing company near our campus. The company has experienced a significant decrease in worker injuries, particularly back injuries, over the past six months. The director of the safety department attributed this improvement to an aerobics instructor he had hired to lead employees in aerobics sessions during breaks. Senior managers were skeptical. My role was to assess the data behind his claim' and also provide additional insights for safety improvements.

After six weeks of analysis, I reached the conclusion that while the aerobics sessions with the cute instructor may have played a partial role, the primary reason for the decrease in injuries was the installation of three new cranes and thousands of dollars worth of associated mechanical lifting devices. These new additions significantly assisted in preventing injuries. Although the safety director was not particularly pleased with my report, he acknowledged the accuracy of my findings.

During the assessment process, the safety director approached me one morning and asked if I wanted to fly to Pittsburgh later that week to visit another headquarters. Despite having a lot of work to do, he assured me that I would be back by nightfall. I was puzzled as to why they would take a lowly college student intern like me, but the safety director explained that they needed three people to use the corporate jet for the trip, and since it was just the two of them going, they would have to fly commercial as was the company's policy. So, they counted me, the unpaid, part-time intern, as the third person.

Near the end of my tenure with this company, I informed the safety director that I was involved in planning a fundraising race for disabled children in a large community center dedicated to their well-being and therapy needs. I mentioned that it was going to be a 10K race and asked if the company would be interested in helping to sponsor the event. He looked at me incredulously and asked in all seriousness, "How the hell can you make kids who are disabled run a 10K race?"

I think that pretty much says it all.

From Elk Hunting to Knee Surgery: A Truly Wild Adventure

Many years ago, a group of ten men went to Idaho to hunt elk. We chose a wilderness area where vehicles were not allowed, so we relied on horses for transportation into the hunting area. We decided to embark on this adventure without guides, but not without thorough preparation beforehand.

On the second day of the hunt, while having lunch about 6 miles from camp, a fellow hunter and I spotted a cow elk (female) at the top of a ridge. During this hunt, you could only shoot males. We devised a plan: I would approach from one direction while he would take another, hoping to see if there was a bull (male) over the ridge. Fortunately, luck was on my side, and I managed to get within 100 yards of a magnificent 6x6 elk. I took my shot and was successful.

Several other hunters from our group came to assist with packing the meat and transporting it back to camp. Being unfamiliar with horseback riding, I found myself in a challenging situation. As darkness approached, the rest of the group headed in one direction while my horse was a mile away in the opposite direction. This was my first experience riding a horse. I was very anxious about riding back to camp in the dark as the light was now fading. So, I ran in the direction of my horse; when I arrived, out of breath, I quickly put my gun in the scabbard and hastily jumped onto the saddle.

With the combination of excitement, exhaustion, and fear, I forgot a very important fact. I was taught that morning that when you leave your horse tied, you should always loosen the saddle for the comfort of the horse.

As I mounted the horse, the saddle slipped, causing the horse pain and bucking, attempting to dislodge the idiot trying to ride her. I knew I was hurting the horse. Just as I was about to let go and drop to the ground, the horse kicked me in my knee. I hit the ground in incredible pain, and I nearly lost consciousness. I watched the horse gallop away. Upon inspecting my right knee, I noticed my kneecap was about 5 inches up my thigh.

Being a hospital CEO but not by any means an orthopedic expert, I assumed I had a dislocated kneecap and tried to push it back into place. Unfortunately, it kept popping back up, indicating a severed patella tendon.

My next concern was whether my walkie-talkie was in my backpack or in the saddlebag that had just disappeared with the horse. Fortunately, I had my walkie-talkie with me, so I radioed my hunting companions for help. They came to my aid, and I stayed at the camp that night. The following day, we embarked on a four-hour drive to a hospital in Montana. There, I received the diagnosis of a ruptured patella tendon that would require surgery.

Now, any sane person would make arrangements to have the surgery at a larger medical center or return home. But I, on the other hand, opted for a brace and decided to return to our hunting camp. As the only one in our group who had successfully shot an elk, and it being an incredible 6x6 Royal elk, I wanted to savor the experience for a few more days with my hunting partners, basking in the male bonding that my occupation did not provide! Two days later, I returned home to my wife, who knew she married a crazy person. Eventually, I underwent surgery back home, and everything turned out well.

Alarm Clock Warning: A Wake-up Call

Many of my healthcare experiences can sometimes feel like "things that never really happened." The story I am about to share with you now fits perfectly into this category.

I worked for an inpatient physical rehabilitation company that was rapidly expanding, opening hospitals nationwide. Within a short period of time, we successfully opened approximately 20 hospitals. I personally assisted in opening three hospitals, one in Arizona and two in Nevada.

While temporarily filling in for a CEO in another city, all 35 rehabilitation hospital CEOs were summoned to a meeting in Chicago. Our flight tickets were provided to ensure that we would all arrive around the same time.

Upon arrival, we were kept in a waiting area outside the conference room at O'Hare Airport. When the time came, we were allowed to enter the room simultaneously. Inside, tables were set up facing the front of the room, with an alarm clock placed at each seating position. We were explicitly instructed not to touch these alarm clocks; the whole thing seemed rather odd.

We patiently waited in silence as our health system CEO and COO stood at the front of the conference room, engaged in conversation. Suddenly, all the alarm clocks went off at the same time.

We were then instructed to turn them off immediately. At that moment, our CEO delivered a brief, 15-minute lecture on our organization's poor financial performance. I believe his exact words were, "These alarms are your f-ing wake-up calls."

After our 15-minute chastisement ended, the CEO bluntly told us to skip the airport bars, get on our planes home, return to our hospitals, and get busy making money or our replacements would……. Not my favorite boss…..

Cannonballs and Parking Woes: Civil War History

While working in hospitals located in states where the Civil War was fought, I had the opportunity to visit historical sites and learn more about the Civil War.

I spent time at a hospital near a Civil War Fort, which was high on a hill. This hospital faced a significant parking problem. Due to a lack of surface parking space, a decision was made to construct an upscale, underground parking garage for our patients on the side of the hill leading up to the hospital. This garage would have an underground tunnel /walkway leading into the hospital.

Around one-third into the construction, workers started discovering cannonballs that had been fired during the Civil War. Construction was immediately halted, and experts in Civil War history and cannonballs were brought in.

It was discovered that most cannonballs fired during the Civil War were solid projectiles, contrary to what is often depicted in movies where cannonballs seem to explode on impact. Occasionally, some cannonballs were filled with black powder that would only explode under high pressure and friction.

The discovered cannonballs were carefully removed, and construction resumed. A total of eight cannonballs were found and safely removed from the site.

However, there was an unintended consequence of this construction. Many of our older patients and their family members, who had either worked in coal mines or had family members working in coal mines, were reluctant to park or walk in a tunnel underground. As a result, the beautiful new parking garage built for our patients and families was predominantly and happily used by employees and physicians.

A Royal Gesture: Taking Care of the Prince

Working in a hospital that doubles as a vacation destination brings numerous advantages. You have the opportunity to meet people from all over the country, and sometimes even from around the world, who visit the area to unwind and appreciate the scenic surroundings.

During one very snowy period, a foreign Prince suffered an ACL tear skiing and expressed his desire to be transported by air to a hospital in Los Angeles for treatment. However, due to heavy and persistent snowfall, it was impossible to arrange a helicopter or fixed-wing aircraft for the Prince's transfer.

As a result, he decided to undergo surgery at our hospital. I had a meeting regarding security with the Prince's handlers/bodyguards, who were all armed with automatic weapons. Obviously curious, I inquired about the reason for carrying such weapons, and their response was straightforward, "There are many people who would like to see the Prince killed."

Naturally, this revelation was unsettling for both me and the staff. Nonetheless, the surgery was successful, and the Prince returned to his local residence to recover.

Several months later, I received an email from the Prince's chief handler expressing the Prince's desire to express gratitude with a gift for our exceptional care and support during his surgery and brief recovery at our hospital.

I gathered our leadership team to brainstorm ideas for what the Prince could contribute to help meet our patient care needs. At the top of our request list was a new 64-slice CT Scanner to replace our outdated 16-slice one.

While we had other less expensive requests, the new CT scan machine was at the top of our request list. Several weeks later, we were informed that the Prince would indeed be donating a brand-new 64-slice CT scan machine to our hospital.

It was ordered, delivered, and installed in 7 months. We were so grateful that we could now provide this improvement in care to our patients and community because of the Prince's generosity and a huge snowstorm.

Medical Tourism: Promises and Pitfalls

For two years, I was a member of the American Association of Medical Tourism Advisory Board. The question I was consistently asked was why I joined such an organization with such a different focus than my existing job description.

My rationale was that a hospital in my region was very close to a major manufacturer that had manufacturing sites overseas. Their executives would often travel to these plants using their corporate jets.

Historically, medical tourism involved patients coming to the US for quality care. However, the impetus for medical tourism shifted when patients started leaving the US for medical care for financial reasons. Many procedures cost significantly less in other countries for very valid reasons. Certain countries and regions began to focus on specific procedures. For example, a resort hospital in Chennai, India, specialized in orthopedics, while clinics and hospitals in Costa Rica focused on dental care and oral surgery.

Initially, individuals going abroad for medical care had to pay in cash upfront. This limited the number of patients who could afford to travel from the US for care. However, my concern arose when selected employers started offering overseas care as an option for employees.

I came across a paper about a paper company in North Carolina that added medical tourism care as an option with benefits for their employees. This study detailed the experience of one of its employees. This employee needed two surgical procedures that were scheduled to be done in Charlotte, North Carolina, with gross charges totaling $190,000. The company was self-insured, so these were going to be their direct costs. The company offered the option of going overseas for care, having already set up arrangements with overseas hospitals and physicians through a medical tourism network. The employee and a physician who would do the procedures in India had completed surgical residencies at Northwestern University Medical School and Baylor. Both had outcome surgical success data similar to major medical centers in the US. Each would meet the patient and spouse on a Zoom call to discuss the treatment plan. If the employee chose this option, the company's costs would approximate:

- Surgical and hospital charges: $55,000
- First-class airfare for the patient and spouse: $10,000
- Resort hotel for the patient and spouse pre- and post-surgery: $3000
- Deposit into the employee's 401(k) account: $20,000

  Total: $88,000   A savings for the company of $102,000

As you can tell, this type of offer would be incredibly appealing to some.

Though still popular in Canada and Europe for quality and wait time reasons, the concept of medical tourism never really caught on in the US, primarily due to concerns about potential complications and issues with insurance coverage when patients returned to the United States.

A Small Hospital's Journey: Covid Challenges

The Covid pandemic impacted us all. New challenges arose for healthcare workers, no matter where they worked – in clinics, large hospitals, small hospitals, home health, or pharmacies. Being a small hospital during COVID-19, we had our own unique challenges, including staffing shortages, difficulty transferring very sick patients to a higher level of care, and difficulties in acquiring personal protective equipment for our employees.

Fear dictated many actions and activities of both the population and employees. One of the community's fears was that going to the hospital increases their risk of catching COVID, despite having all safety measures, infection control, and regulations in place, making it really the safest place in the community.

One of the greatest hardships we faced as a small hospital was not being able to allow visitors during the pandemic; this was especially painful for families and friends of terminally ill patients.

Being a small hospital, we lacked an intensive care unit, making it challenging to care for critically ill patients. Our struggle involved trying to find hospitals with available intensive care beds to transfer our patients for proper care. This issue became a significant national news story.

David Muir, the host of ABC Evening News, visited our small hospital and interviewed me in one of our emergency rooms to discuss the situation and the challenges we encountered, including the personal tragedies associated with the inability to transfer patients to a higher level of care.

The outcomes of COVID-19 varied dramatically. In our hospital, we witnessed a patient under 40 with no underlying health conditions succumb to COVID-19. Conversely, during the same month, we had a patient over 100 years old diagnosed with

COVID and pneumonia, who was effectively treated and happily returned home to their family, where the patient lived another 14 months.

9 798223 851141